Frédéric Delalot

washingtonias and zoetropes 11

KDP Editions

Panting beach...
Summaries onwards
Exchanged...

Against pleasures...
The century unfolds
Endlessly...

From July...
From elsewhere
A revival.

This impression...

Of light opium...

Enjoy the bodies...

In the hands of carousels

Footage...

Sounds...

Totality...

Meetings

Absolute...

Cross...

Gymnics...

Out of time.

In the perfect heat...

To stroll...

Large number of years

I was trying to understand

Discovering

Cities...

And seaside

Of course...

On the other side

Weekends

Sometimes distance

Place, quay...

Quebec Palace

Of sand...

Which was drying up...

Nomads...

From the beach, transcendence...

Docks, ecstasy...

There are areas of transparency

Flawless consistency...

Light creates a sanctuary

Beyond friendship...

To accompany my nights

In North America...

The eras...

Chalk on one of the tables...

Thin strip of sand...

Balance had its source

Behind a tree of the square

Preserved me...

Close to beaches

Appointment...

Hanging...

In bubbles...

After years...

I saw landscapes

Distant...

Drought...

When we walked

Indefinite din...

Thousands of worlds

I loved the exaltation...

We could see the city...

Inner courtyards, elongated

The days began...

A long time ago...

Unforgettable music

Some nights...

Another planet...

Attractive lights

And stone facades...

Same old quarter

From then on, magnetizations.

This is the way we had found

Possess a few moments...

Blurry punctuations...

I saw people

Flying over the street...

Emotional prism

At the heart of the years

Stories...

Delusional feats.

Show...

Out of the ordinary...

In the azure space...

In Paris, there was an inner courtyard

There was simply fun

To walk in the city...

From the time...

There was the crowd of the Night...

Maybe because of the beaches

We were a caravan...

I remembered a look

Fairground atmosphere...

Rhythm of caresses...

This certain speed...

There were deserted beaches

Possible, sometimes...

I wanted to spread out my time

Purple lights...

Indistinct...

Ah! the summer like no other...

Driving cars

Lagoons...

Rides...

Truce plants...

A thousand years...

Separate us

Reminiscences

Faces...

Caresses...

Screens, the wheel...

Things...

Sometimes, yielding to the imperceptible

Tram turns...

All this in a big circle...

The world was going...

Erotic...

Elusive moments.

Growing track

Unrealities...

Requirements...

Simultaneous...

Hacienda

Maybe

Rhythms

Jerky

There were words...

After several years

Suns...

From an island...

Towards horizons...

Mesmerizing...

We are energy

Laurels of the field...

Doors...

Towers...

Outskirts...

Wonders

About ten seconds

Review each chapter...

There were young people...

Habits...

A long time ago...

In the herbs...

Branches of a pine tree

Giant...

After all...

Idyllic surface...

Where there is a logic

What do you want...

Like wanderings

Parisian ceilings...

Fluctuating carousel

Naked waves...

Synthetic...

Then came the casuals

The summer sky...

Spread out its order...

Distances...

Diamonds to join

Huge sky...

The order of things

Variability

Partition...

Enjoyment

Geodetic...

Seconds...

Unexpectedly

Variances...

Spheres...

Human project

Domain in the sun

Elliptic...

At the opening...

There is a total book

We perceive its currents

We'll cross paths...

Over there...

By a tour of ideas...

Cove, flowers

At birth

Waves...

Aloof...

Happy night

Informed...

Fast...

Other places...

Change...

Maybe a canvas

In time...

Impressions of the night

Laughing look...

Feelings of then...

Cause of all sequels

The pace drove...

To the uneven way...

Lost in thought...

Stealthy looks...

Stops, night races

Splendor of a love...

The meaning of this momentum is distant...

Inaccessible, warm reunion

Many fall asleep, lie down

Life stretches...

Nascent fantasy...

Back to the West

Delusional immensity

Let him contemplate...

Montreal...

To the point of exaltation

By some instinct

Promptly...

In Paris, passion...

Rue des Taillandiers

American T-shirt...

Crew...

At the top...

And on the banks...

It's nice to believe...

That we are beings

From the ordinary...

There are so many reasons

Which immortalize...

Power of lovers

Yellowed veils...

Anonymous headlights...

Cars...

In the corners...

As long as the show was going.

First imagination

Tier of bookstores...

Instinctive fortune...

Exist elsewhere...

Floral emblems...

Buildings...

She was cavalier, hippie...

We were moped

I don't know where it comes from...

Nor where she leaves, seasons, parties

There was a shortcut...

An obvious present, of trophies.

Virtually accessible

Inner path...

Packing of atriums

Apostrophe...

Slightly vague...

Feeling of the months

Honey ponds...

Invisible...

Of a supreme leisure

Nude images...

And attracting revival...

So many months...

Since our temptations...

We were walks...

From a prepared planet

Memorable...

8

On platforms...

A fraction of a second

With suggestive poses...

Colors get carried away

Strong alcohol...

Generous dimensions...

A mirror reflects

Mesmerizing, docked...

In a harbor...

Surrealist globality

At every moment...

Brown of Mercury...

Lagoons...

Under olive trees...

I think, constantly...

To a larger change

There are strange empires...

Lost at the edge

Known seas...

Pleasures...

Land...

Holiday track...

Paris periphery...

Before the Opera...

We were walking in the streets

The rest of the world seems far away...

Almost unreal, will we see the other side again

By I don't know what mirobolant magic

Elsewhere, next to reality...

Ephemeral mixture...

Rasades, remote memories

Escapes the wandering era...

In a set...

Colors of the alarm clock...

The other day, again...

I noticed many hitches

As in the year one thousand...

9

Stars that we contemplate...

In a rear-view mirror, on the road

Knowing that summer is moving away...

Maybe Empire...

Encompassing nomads

Close to the shores...

On this planet of lines...

Obscure blotter, good times...

Out of the doubt, perfect sequences.

Previous trips...

Glory of flags

Order of lineages...

To get there...

Shadows and dust...

Their design, we took over...

Timeless of research, happiness...

These lights were advancing, above the mountains

Euphoria, alone in the drunken night...

Continents in osmosis, during these months

And the locomotive went astray in times...

Far from it that this world does win...

Huge plants...

Perfect times...

Hypnotic detachment

The color of the posters...

From the eyes of others...

Carefree page, rebel...

Rough hair, philosophers

Pleasant wanderings, a fortiori...

Like an echo...

The landscapes are changing...

Summer, at the heart of promises

Eternity by the contours...

And this landscape is ours...

In front of me, so many hugs...

Have I not dreamed of millennia

At the end of the clouds...

Sky of Spain...

Flippapered notebooks

Introspection...

Fantasies of impatience

To the climax...

So many other games...

Transforming time...

Offshore, the form of the narrative

So much and more...

Creation...

Behind the peaks...

From a height of view

Untraceable...

Like others...

I was hoping for a merger...

Something alchemical...

We are only a moment

As we arrive

To believe in a dream...

Sometimes, swirling

Nested worlds.

Circles...

From the world...

Our trip

Apart...

Clothes on the cushions

The horizon loves us...

So to speak...

Mysterious energies...

Garden of dreams...

By episodes, always...

The clear waves are drunk

With other archives...

Printing, advances...

Unless you've dreamed of these things

The sets remember...

Epics, foreign cities.

She adjusted her hours

From the century...

Interior spaces...

Twists in the parks...

After the linen sails...

She liked to unveil a repeated sequence

Choosing the equipped...

Our distances, the mix

The azure rocks...

Quiet festival

All these images

Bird Squares

Wonderful energies

That's right...

Perhaps it was necessary to abstain...

To think, at your fingertips...

I just organized menus

Bourgeois conquest

On the sanitized coasts

Alchemy, attraction...

Pleasant stimulation.

From a beach...

In the place of our gallant Indies

The spiral sensation of an order

Wandering, in the enigmatic glow...

From the heavens...

Prime youth...

Precious years...

What could the empire offer me

And like a curious nothing

Clones of variations...

Golden plots...

Bird flights...

Exterior stairs...

Even if nothing changes

Oh, really...

Apart from the landscapes...

In Paris...

Crazy sauteries

Rainy clouds...

After one kilometer

Brushing...

Summer settings...

The Hexagon...

Different environments

Ancient banners...

Subtropical canvases

In front of the Opera...

Nomadic trinkets...

I click...

Unprecedented latitude...

Eleventh arrondissement

The falling wick...

Undefined places...

Constant pretext...

Cosmopolitan crowd

Perfect rhythms...

Carefree...

Shuddered...

Above screens

Erotic, incongruous

Island logic...

Escape from countries...

Unreal, humble humans

We were meeting space

Pictorial, canvas of culture

Drunk...

Embraced with sensations...

Collective...

Sublimated to the song of the waves

From the Anse...

Stories of fantasies...

Wouldn't we hold back...

Only two or three sequences.

13

Orgasm later

Rear machine...

Superimposed realities

Visitor of pinnacles...

I had returned to the sets

Their sumptuous angles...

Attraction of light...

Magmatic ornament...

Sometimes, absolute purpose.

A kind of symbolic levitation

Reproducing figures...

Innovative imagination...

From hour to hour...

Depending on the location...

Wandering charm

Part of dream...

Scattered disorders

Perfect position of the fold

Through time...

At will...

Free posture...

There was a union

With nature...

Finally, at dawn...

Lifting the sand...

When they had been shores

Whole...

And steps...

Dreamlike...

Sometimes...

The world was born

Promises...

Between the facades...

Bricks...

New beginnings

In pieces of sky...

Expanses...

14

On a higher stone...

Which came out of the water, a little leaning

You abandoned yourself...

Like a lighthouse...

Opium direction...

I see the swirling sand

The heart of the action, forgotten...

And these gigantic beaches...

Brought us to the detours.

South waves...

We had a shortcut

Nuances of projects...

That we liked...

Something was going on...

Superb creatures, exuberant mix

A microcosm...

We ignored the reflections...

Knowing that there were many orgasms...

Flavors of the island's song, a presence...

In fact, but from an outlying position

Covered in visionary colors...

We were talking about it...

Memorable day...

Launching its rounds...

Echoing the wonders

In the azure...

Indian caresses...

The fluid kept us going

In suspension...

We went, panting...

In plant heat

With this impression...

Touching, docile...

In high season...

Overflowing with the assembly

There was a happiness...

To perceive emotion.

15

Fading fountains faded

Notepad of wishes, artistic blur...

At the height of dawn...

And summer, which is ours...

In the fun...

Color of cities, often

Replaced false happiness

Off the road...

I integrated myself into these possibilities.

Waves of ecstasy...

Wave of moments...

Did we understand anything

To this ribbon of instincts...

From the dark to the azure anchor...

There, colors of the tip

Sunny, pages...

Scorching story...

And I was wondering...

Near the huge cacti...

I remembered, precisely...

The vertiginous atmospheres.

Pampered streets...

The best of every era

In this cheerful conjunction...

Amazing...

Leaning trees...

Sun licking...

Near the tans...

Nightingale or Elephant

And the summer...

Intoxicating gold, nomadic ...

New days, constantly heroes

Can we only glimpse them...

When the walls are adorned...

Mirrors and colors...

Crossing hypnotic glows

Perfect suite...

16

Touch in the evening, like an altitude

Start again, perhaps...

Gets drunk the machine to enrich...

In the high bays...

Figures that are given

In the jubilation...

Transparencies cuts...

Magic of adding the days...

Perhaps, quest for peace.

Unimaginable world...

In another dimension...

New York...

And the muscles of an Apache

Hope invites me...

Which creates the appeal...

Adventure lover

Hacienda...

Never mind the ballet

From the day before...

Capital with palavers...

In the center of the rounds.

A twist...

Had buried...

Apart from the foam

Atlantean fauna

Without waiting...

These exiles intoxicated...

Even the sky of empires

To the theatre...

Alleys...

Wild...

Interfered...

In precious nature

Simple seasons...

Behind the ramparts...

Smooth stone screens

On the outskirts of foreign...

17

Historical...

Soporific...

Pale figures

Then...

Reversible trips

Mysterious clarity...

Impression...

Amazing...

Hugs.

Height...

Immediately shiny

Indecisive chimeras

Transformed parties

We were waiting for infinity

Posters of indifference

Our summer evenings...

I envied you my nights

Foolish...

Our fuzzy chaos

Of boudragues...

Up to the port...

Absolute suns...

Heights...

Mutants...

Mind-boggling pleasure

Of these earthly excesses

Rides...

Dried leaves...

Revolutions...

The wind was smoothing...

Our hair...

Under haunting fabrics

The evening we contemplate...

With the gold of images...

According to the sails...

Ephemeral, of a summer

And the enthusiasm...

18

Windows...

Carousel...

Drunk boat

And hot places...

Same curtains drawn...

I was waiting like this

Scrolls...

Bright houses...

I liked other ways.

We'll even laugh...

Nowadays...

When these felonous hordes

Will have ruined the earth...

Invincible...

Jubilation...

Unequivocal

In the sea...

Ideas...

Designs...

Inexplicable path

Chance...

Forge of the world

I am writing to you...

Far from the coast...

Soothing ink...

Between these poles...

Crossing arches...

Separation of gravity

At the perfect line...

In the heart...

Lines...

In the light

Intense...

Book to the limits...

Of the Order...

Arches...

Hallucinogenic oil.

19

Nascent fantasy...

There are so many reasons

Exist elsewhere...

Since our temptations...

With suggestive poses...

There are strange empires

Escapes the wandering era...

Obscure blotter, good times...

Euphoria, alone in the drunken night.

In front of me, so many hugs...

Fantasies of impatience...

Something alchemical...

Unless you've dreamed of these things

She liked to unveil a repeated sequence

Pleasant stimulation...

What could the empire offer me...

In different environments...

Subtropical canvases...

Stories of fantasies

From the pinnacles...

Free posture...

Finally, at dawn...

Opium direction...

Knowing that there were many orgasms

The fluid kept us...

In the fun...

Ribbon of instincts...

Hypnotic glows...

Start over, maybe

Hope invites me

Sky of empires...

Reversible trips...

Summer evenings...

Under haunting fabrics

I was waiting like this...

Unequivocal...

Far from the coast...